ESSENTIAL
Pasta

P

Contents

Introduction

Pasta is one of the earliest culinary inventions and dates back as far as the second century BC. Italy and pasta may seem synonymous, however pasta-making traditions have been traced in countries other than Italy, such as China, Mongolia, Greece, Spain, Israel, and Russia.

It was commonly thought that Marco Polo brought the art of pasta-making to Italy after his travels in China. However, it is now recognised that he was already familiar with pasta before travelling to China as it was first made by the Etruscans in central Italy in 500 BC.

Regardless of its origin, pasta is now a worldwide favourite. Not only is it nutritious, it is cheap and extremely versatile too. For those with a busy lifestyle, pasta made from durum wheat which contains protein and carbohydrates, is a great energy provider and takes just a few minutes to cook.

It is a good idea to always have a supply of dried pasta, such as rigatoni, spaghetti or perhaps fusilli in your cupboard, as it can be cooked quickly and added to pasta sauce for a tasty meal. Alternatively you can buy fresh pasta from your delicatessen or local supermarket. However, be careful when choosing fresh pasta.

It is generally more expensive than the dried alternative and is usually not any better. In fact, fresh pasta often contains lower levels of protein than dried pasta and can be less absorbent and more starchy.

There are as many as 200 different types of pasta to choose from, in various shapes and sizes, and all can be combined with fish, meat, poultry, vegetables, herbs or even fruit to create delicious appetising meals.

To make a basic pasta dough at home use 450 g/1 lb/4 cups durum wheat flour, 4 lightly beaten eggs and 1 tbsp of olive oil with a pinch of salt. On a lightly floured surface, sift the flour and salt into a mound. Make a well in the middle and add the eggs and olive oil. Use a fork or your fingers to gradually work the mixture until the ingredients are combined and knead for 10–15 minutes. Set the dough aside to rest for 25 minutes, before rolling it out as thinly as possible.

Pasta should be cooked in lightly salted boiling water until it is tender yet firm to the bite. The Italians call this *al dente* (to the tooth). Dried unfilled pasta takes 8–12 minutes; fresh unfilled pasta takes 2–3 minutes; dried filled pasta takes 15–20 minutes; fresh filled pasta takes 8–10 minutes. To prevent sticking and to enhance flavour add a tablespoon of olive oil to the boiling water. Once the pasta is cooked, drain it in a colander and serve with sauce.

Chorizo & Wild Mushrooms with a Spicy Vermicelli

Serves 6

INGREDIENTS

680 g/1^1/$_2$ lb dried vermicelli
125 ml/4 fl oz/^{1}/$_2$ cup olive oil
2 garlic cloves
125 g/4^1/$_2$ oz chorizo, sliced

225 g/8 oz wild mushrooms
3 fresh red chillies, chopped
2 tbsp freshly grated
  Parmesan cheese

salt and pepper
10 anchovy fillets, to garnish

1 Bring a large pan of lightly salted water to the boil. Add the vermicelli and 1 tbsp of the oil and cook until just tender, but still firm to the bite. Drain, place on a warm serving plate and keep warm.

2 Meanwhile heat the remaining oil in a large frying pan (skillet). Add the garlic and fry for 1 minute. Add the chorizo and wild mushrooms and cook for 4 minutes, then add the chopped chillies and cook for 1 further minute.

3 Pour the chorizo and wild mushroom mixture over the vermicelli and season. Sprinkle over the freshly grated Parmesan cheese, garnish with a lattice of anchovy fillets and serve immediately.

VARIATION

Fresh sardines may be used instead of the anchovies. However, ensure that you gut and clean the sardines, removing the backbone, before using them.

COOK'S TIP

Always obtain wild mushrooms from a reliable source: never pick them yourself unless you are sure of their identity. Many varieties of mushrooms are now cultivated and most are indistinguishable from the wild varieties. Mixed colour oyster mushrooms are used here, but you could also use chanterelles. However, chanterelles shrink during cooking, so you may need more.

Orecchiette with Bacon & Tomatoes

Serves 4

INGREDIENTS

900 g/2 lb small, sweet
  tomatoes
6 slices rindless, smoked bacon
60 g/2 oz/4 tbsp butter
1 onion, chopped

1 garlic clove, crushed
4 fresh oregano sprigs,
  finely chopped
450 g/1 lb/4 cups dried
  orecchiette

1 tbsp olive oil
salt and pepper
fresh basil sprigs, to garnish
freshly grated Pecorino
  cheese, to serve

1 Blanch the tomatoes in boiling water. Drain, skin and seed the tomatoes, then roughly chop the flesh. Chop the bacon into small dice.

2 Melt the butter in a saucepan and fry the bacon until it is golden. Add the onion and garlic and fry for 5-7 minutes, until softened.

3 Add the tomatoes and oregano to the pan and season to taste. Lower the heat and simmer for 10-12 minutes.

4 Bring a pan of lightly salted water to the boil. Add the orecchiette and oil and cook for 12 minutes, until just tender, but still firm to the bite. Drain and transfer to a serving dish. Spoon over the bacon and tomato sauce and toss to coat. Garnish and serve.

VARIATION

You could also use 450 g/ 1 lb spicy Italian sausages. Squeeze the meat out of the skins and add to the pan in step 2 instead of the bacon.

COOK'S TIP

For an authentic Italian flavour use pancetta, rather than ordinary bacon. This kind of bacon is streaked with fat and adds rich undertones of flavour to many traditional dishes. It is available both smoked and unsmoked and can be bought in a single, large piece or cut into slices. You can buy it in some supermarkets and all Italian delicatessens.

Sicilian Spaghetti

Serves 4

INGREDIENTS

150 ml/¼ pint/⅝ cup olive
 oil, plus extra for brushing
2 aubergines (eggplants)
350 g/12 oz/3 cups minced
 (ground) beef
1 onion, chopped
2 garlic cloves, crushed
2 tbsp tomato purée (paste)

400 g/14 oz can chopped
 tomatoes
1 tsp Worcestershire sauce
1 tsp chopped fresh marjoram
 or oregano or ½ tsp dried
 marjoram or oregano
60 g/2 oz/½ cup stoned
 (pitted) black olives, sliced

1 green, red or yellow (bell)
 pepper, cored, seeded and
 chopped
175 g/6 oz dried spaghetti
115 g/4 oz/1 cup freshly
 grated Parmesan cheese
salt and pepper

1 Brush a 20 cm/8 inch loose-based round cake tin (pan) with oil, line the base with baking parchment and brush with oil.

2 Slice the aubergines (eggplants). Fry the aubergines (eggplants) in a little oil until browned on both sides. Drain on kitchen paper (towels).

3 Cook the beef, onion and garlic in a pan, stirring, until browned. Add the tomato purée (paste), tomatoes, Worcestershire sauce, herbs and salt and pepper. Simmer for 10 minutes. Add the olives and (bell) pepper and cook for a further 10 minutes.

4 Bring a pan of salted water to the boil. Add the spaghetti and 1 tbsp olive oil and cook until tender. Drain and turn the spaghetti into a bowl. Add the meat mixture and cheese and toss to mix.

5 Arrange aubergine (eggplant) slices over the base and sides of the tin (pan). Add the pasta, then cover with the rest of the aubergine (eggplant). Bake in a preheated oven at 200°C/400°F/ Gas 6 for 40 minutes. Leave to stand for 5 minutes, then invert on to a serving dish. Discard the baking parchment and serve.

Lasagne Verde

Serves 4–6

INGREDIENTS

butter, for greasing
14 sheets pre-cooked lasagne
850 ml/1^1/2 pints/3^3/4 cups
    Béchamel Sauce
75 g/3 oz/^{3}/4 cup grated
    mozzarella cheese
fresh basil (optional), to
    garnish

MEAT SAUCE:
25 ml/1 fl oz/^{1}/8 cup olive oil
450 g/1 lb/4 cups minced
    (ground) beef
1 large onion, chopped
1 celery stick (stalk), diced
4 cloves garlic, crushed
25g/1 oz/^{1}/4 cup plain
    (all purpose) flour

300 ml/^{1}/2 pint/1^1/4 cups beef
    stock
150 ml/^{1}/4 pint/^{5}/8 cup red
    wine
1 tbsp chopped fresh parsley
1 tsp chopped fresh marjoram
1 tsp chopped fresh basil
2 tbsp tomato purée (paste)
salt and pepper

1 To make the meat sauce, heat the olive oil in a large frying pan (skillet). Add the minced (ground) beef and fry, stirring frequently, until browned all over. Add the onion, celery and garlic and cook for 3 minutes.

2 Sprinkle over the flour and cook, stirring constantly, for 1 minute. Gradually stir in the stock and red wine. Season well and add the parsley, marjoram and basil. Bring to the boil, lower the heat and simmer for 35 minutes. Add the tomato purée (paste) and simmer for a further 10 minutes.

3 Lightly grease an ovenproof dish with butter. Arrange sheets of lasagne over the base of the dish, spoon over a layer of meat sauce, then Béchamel Sauce. Place another layer of lasagne on top and repeat the process twice, finishing with a layer of Béchamel Sauce. Sprinkle over the grated mozzarella cheese.

4 Bake the lasagne in a preheated oven at 190°C/375°F/Gas 5 for 35 minutes, until the top is golden brown and bubbling. Garnish with fresh basil, if liked, and serve immediately.

Pasticcio

Serves 6

INGREDIENTS

250 g/8 oz/2 cups dried fusilli

1 tbsp olive oil, plus extra
for brushing

4 tbsp double (heavy) cream

mixed salad, to serve

SAUCE:

2 tbsp olive oil

1 onion, thinly sliced

1 red (bell) pepper, cored,
seeded and chopped

2 garlic cloves, chopped

600 g/1 lb 5 oz/5$\frac{1}{4}$ cups
minced (ground) beef

400 g/14 oz can chopped
tomatoes

125 ml/4 fl oz/$\frac{1}{2}$ cup dry
white wine

2 tbsp chopped fresh parsley

60 g/2 oz can anchovies,
drained and chopped

salt and pepper

TOPPING:

300 ml/$\frac{1}{2}$ pint/1$\frac{1}{4}$ cups
natural yogurt

3 eggs

pinch of freshly grated
nutmeg

40 g/1$\frac{1}{2}$ oz/$\frac{1}{2}$ cup freshly
grated Parmesan cheese

1 To make the sauce, heat the oil in a frying pan (skillet) and fry the onion and red (bell) pepper for 3 minutes. Add the garlic and cook for 1 minute. Add the beef and cook until browned.

2 Add the tomatoes and wine and bring to the boil. Simmer for 20 minutes, until thickened.

Stir in the parsley, anchovies and seasoning.

3 Bring a pan of salted water to the boil. Add the pasta and oil and cook for 10 minutes, until almost tender. Drain and transfer to a bowl. Stir in the cream.

4 For the topping, beat together the yogurt, eggs and nutmeg.

5 Brush an ovenproof dish with oil. Spoon in half the pasta and cover with half the meat sauce. Repeat, then spread over the topping and sprinkle with cheese.

6 Bake in a preheated oven at 190°C/375°F/ Gas 5 for 25 minutes until golden. Serve with a mixed salad.

Neapolitan Veal Cutlets with Mascarpone Cheese & Marille

Serves 4

INGREDIENTS

200 g/7 oz/^{7}/$_8$ cup butter

4 x 250 g/9 oz veal cutlets, trimmed

1 large onion, sliced

2 apples, peeled, cored and sliced

175 g/6 oz button mushrooms

1 tbsp chopped fresh tarragon

8 black peppercorns

1 tbsp sesame seeds

400 g/14 oz dried marille

100 ml/3^1/$_2$ fl oz/scant ^{1}/$_2$ cup extra virgin olive oil

175 g/6 oz/^{3}/$_4$ cup mascarpone cheese, broken into small pieces

salt and pepper

2 large beef tomatoes, cut in half

leaves of 1 fresh basil sprig

1 Melt 60 g/2 oz/4 tbsp of the butter in a frying pan (skillet). Gently fry the veal for 5 minutes on each side. Transfer to a dish and keep warm.

2 Fry the onion and apples until golden. Transfer to a dish, top with the veal and keep warm.

3 Fry the mushrooms, tarragon and peppercorns in the remaining butter for 3 minutes. Sprinkle over the sesame seeds.

4 Bring a pan of salted water to the boil. Add the pasta and 1 tbsp of the oil and cook until tender. Drain and transfer to a serving plate.

5 Top the pasta with the cheese and sprinkle over the remaining olive oil. Place the onions, apples and veal cutlets on top of the pasta. Spoon the mushrooms, peppercorns and pan juices on to the cutlets, place the tomatoes and basil leaves around the edge of the plate and place in a preheated oven at 150°C/300°F/Gas 2 for 5 minutes. Season to taste with salt and pepper and serve immediately.

Stuffed Cannelloni

Serves 4

INGREDIENTS

8 dried cannelloni tubes
1 tbsp olive oil
25 g/1 oz/$^{1}/_{4}$ cup freshly
    grated Parmesan cheese
fresh herb sprigs, to garnish

FILLING:
25 g/1 oz/2 tbsp butter
300 g/10$^{1}/_{2}$ oz frozen spinach,
    thawed and chopped

115 g/4 oz/1$^{1}/_{2}$ cup ricotta
    cheese
25 g/1 oz/$^{1}/_{4}$ cup freshly
    grated Parmesan cheese
60 g/2 oz/$^{1}/_{4}$ cup chopped
    ham
pinch of freshly grated
    nutmeg
2 tbsp double (heavy) cream
2 eggs, lightly beaten

salt and pepper

SAUCE:
25 g/1 oz/2 tbsp butter
25 g/1 oz/$^{1}/_{4}$ cup plain
    (all purpose) flour
300 ml/$^{1}/_{2}$ pint/1$^{1}/_{4}$ cups milk
2 bay leaves
pinch of freshly grated
    nutmeg

1 For the filling, melt the butter in a pan and stir-fry the spinach for 2–3 minutes. Remove from the heat and stir in the cheeses and the ham. Season with nutmeg, salt and pepper. Beat in the cream and eggs to make a thick paste.

2 Cook the pasta with the oil in a pan of salted boiling water until tender. Drain and set aside.

3 To make the sauce, melt the butter in a pan. Stir in the flour and cook for 1 minute. Gradually stir in the milk and the bay leaves and simmer for 5 minutes. Add the nutmeg and seasoning. Remove from the heat and discard the bay leaves.

4 Spoon the filling into a piping bag and fill the cannelloni.

5 Spoon a little sauce into the base of an ovenproof dish. Arrange the cannelloni in the dish in a single layer and pour over the remaining sauce. Sprinkle over the Parmesan cheese and bake in a preheated oven at 190°C/375°F/Gas 5 for about 40–45 minutes. Garnish with the fresh herb sprigs and serve immediately.

Tagliatelle with Pumpkin

Serves 4

INGREDIENTS

500 g/1 lb 2 oz pumpkin or
  butternut squash, peeled
  and seeded
3 tbsp olive oil
1 onion, finely chopped
2 garlic cloves, crushed
4–6 tbsp chopped fresh
  parsley

pinch of freshly grated
  nutmeg
about 250 ml/9 fl oz/1$\frac{1}{4}$ cups
  chicken or vegetable stock
115 g/4 oz Parma ham
  (prosciutto)
250 g/9 oz dried tagliatelle

150 ml/$\frac{1}{4}$ pint/$\frac{5}{8}$ cup double
  (heavy cream)
salt and pepper
freshly grated Parmesan
  cheese, to serve

1 Cut the pumpkin or butternut squash in half and scoop out the seeds. Cut the flesh into 1 cm/$\frac{1}{2}$ inch dice.

2 Heat 2 tbsp of the olive oil in a large saucepan and fry the onion and garlic over a low heat for about 3 minutes, until soft. Add half the parsley and fry for 1 minute.

3 Add the pumpkin or squash pieces and cook for 2–3 minutes. Season to taste with salt, pepper and nutmeg.

4 Add half the stock to the pan, bring to the boil, cover and simmer for 10 minutes, or until the pumpkin or squash is tender, adding more stock if necessary.

5 Add the Parma ham (prosciutto) to the pan and cook, stirring frequently, for 2 minutes.

6 Bring a large pan of lightly salted water to the boil. Add the tagliatelle and the remaining oil and cook for 12 minutes, until tender, but still firm to the bite. Drain and transfer to a warm serving dish.

7 Stir the cream into the pumpkin and ham mixture and heat through. Spoon over the pasta, sprinkle over the remaining parsley and serve immediately.

Tagliatelle with Chicken Sauce

Serves 4

INGREDIENTS

250 g/9 oz fresh green
   tagliatelle
1 tbsp olive oil
fresh basil leaves, to garnish
salt

TOMATO SAUCE:
2 tbsp olive oil
1 small onion, chopped
1 garlic clove, chopped

400 g/14 oz can chopped
   tomatoes
2 tbsp chopped fresh parsley
1 tsp dried oregano
2 bay leaves
2 tbsp tomato purée (paste)
1 tsp sugar
salt and pepper

CHICKEN SAUCE:
60 g/2 oz/4 tbsp unsalted
   butter
400 g/14 oz boned chicken
   breasts, skinned and cut
   into thin strips
90 g/3 oz/^{3}/$_4$ cup blanched
   almonds
300 ml/^{1}/$_2$ pint/1^1/$_4$ cups
   double (heavy) cream
salt and pepper

1 To make the tomato sauce, heat the oil and fry the onion until translucent. Add the garlic and fry for 1 minute. Stir in the tomatoes, herbs, tomato purée (paste), sugar and seasoning to taste. Bring to the boil and simmer for 15–20 minutes, until reduced by half. Remove from the heat and discard the bay leaves.

2 To make the chicken sauce, melt the butter in a frying pan (skillet) and stir-fry the chicken and almonds for 5–6 minutes, until the chicken is cooked.

3 Meanwhile, bring the cream to the boil over a low heat for about 10 minutes, until reduced by half. Pour the cream over the chicken and almonds,

stir and season to taste. Set aside and keep warm.

4 Bring a pan of salted water to the boil. Add the tagliatelle and olive oil and cook until tender. Drain and transfer to a warm serving dish. Spoon over the tomato sauce and arrange the chicken sauce on top. Garnish with the basil leaves and serve.

Tortellini

Serves 4

INGREDIENTS

115 g/4 oz boned chicken
　breast, skinned
60 g/2 oz Parma ham
　(prosciutto)
40 g/1$^{1}/_{2}$ oz cooked spinach,
　well drained
1 tbsp finely chopped onion
2 tbsp freshly grated
　Parmesan cheese

pinch of ground allspice
1 egg, beaten
450 g/1 lb Basic Pasta Dough
salt and pepper
2 tbsp chopped fresh parsley,
　to garnish

SAUCE:
300 ml/$^{1}/_{2}$ pint/1$^{1}/_{4}$ cups
　single (light) cream
2 garlic cloves, crushed
115 g/4 oz button mushrooms,
　thinly sliced
4 tbsp freshly grated
　Parmesan cheese

1 Bring a pan of seasoned water to the boil. Add the chicken and poach for 10 minutes. Cool slightly, then process in a food processor, with the Parma ham (prosciutto), spinach and onion until finely chopped. Stir in the Parmesan cheese, allspice and egg and season to taste.

2 Thinly roll out the pasta dough and cut into 5 cm/2 inch rounds.

3 Place ½ tsp of the filling in the centre of each round. Fold the pieces in half and press the edges to seal. Then wrap each piece around your index finger, cross over the ends and curl the rest of the dough backwards to make a navel shape.

4 Bring a pan of salted water to the boil. Add the tortellini, bring back to the boil and cook for

5 minutes. Drain and transfer to a serving dish.

5 To make the sauce, bring the cream and garlic to the boil then simmer for 3 minutes. Add the mushrooms and half the cheese, season and simmer for 2–3 minutes. Pour the sauce over the tortellini. Sprinkle over the remaining Parmesan, garnish with the parsley and serve.

46

Chicken with Green Olives & Pasta

Serves 4

INGREDIENTS

4 chicken breasts, part boned
3 tbsp olive oil
25 g/1 oz/2 tbsp butter
1 large onion, finely chopped
2 garlic cloves, crushed
2 red, yellow or green (bell)
    peppers, cored, seeded and
    cut into large pieces

250 g/9 oz button
    mushrooms, sliced or
    quartered
175 g/6 oz tomatoes, skinned
    and halved
150 ml/$\frac{1}{4}$ pint/$\frac{5}{8}$ cup dry
    white wine

175 g/6 oz/1$\frac{1}{2}$ cups stoned
    (pitted) green olives
4–6 tbsp double (heavy) cream
400 g/14 oz dried pasta
salt and pepper
chopped parsley, to garnish

1 Fry the chicken breasts in 2 tbsp of the oil and the butter until golden brown. Remove the chicken from the pan.

2 Add the onion and garlic to the pan and fry until beginning to soften. Add the (bell) peppers and mushrooms and cook for 2–3 minutes. Add the tomatoes and seasoning. Transfer the vegetables to a casserole with the chicken.

3 Add the wine to the pan and bring to the boil. Pour the wine over the chicken. Cover and cook in a preheated oven at 180°C/350°F/Gas 4 for 50 minutes.

4 Mix the olives into the casserole. Pour in the cream, cover and return to the oven for 10–20 minutes.

5 Meanwhile, bring a large pan of lightly salted water to the boil. Add the pasta and the remaining oil and cook until tender, but still firm to the bite. Drain the pasta well and transfer to a serving dish.

6 Arrange the chicken on top of the pasta, spoon over the sauce, garnish with the parsley and serve immediately. Alternatively, place the pasta in a large serving bowl and serve separately.

Rigatoni & Pesto Baked Partridge

Serves 4

INGREDIENTS

8 partridge pieces
  (about 115 g/4 oz each)
60 g/2 oz/4 tbsp butter, melted
4 tbsp Dijon mustard
2 tbsp lime juice

1 tbsp brown sugar
6 tbsp Pesto Sauce
450 g/1 lb dried rigatoni
1 tbsp olive oil

115 g/4 oz/1$^{1}/_{3}$ cups freshly
  grated Parmesan cheese
salt and pepper

1 Arrange the partridge pieces, smooth side down, in a single layer in a large, ovenproof dish.

2 Mix together the butter, Dijon mustard, lime juice and brown sugar in a bowl. Season to taste. Brush the mixture over the upper surfaces of the partridge pieces and bake in a preheated oven at 200°C/400°F/Gas 6 for 15 minutes.

3 Remove the dish from the oven and coat the partridge pieces with 3 tbsp of the Pesto Sauce. Return to the oven and bake for a further 12 minutes.

4 Remove the dish from the oven and carefully turn over the partridge pieces. Coat the top of the partridges with the remaining mustard mixture and return to the oven for a further 10 minutes.

5 Meanwhile, bring a large saucepan of lightly salted water to the boil. Add the rigatoni and olive oil and cook for about 10 minutes until tender, but still firm to the bite. Drain and transfer to a serving dish. Toss the pasta with the remaining Pesto Sauce and the Parmesan.

6 Arrange the pieces of partridge on the serving dish with the rigatoni, pour over the cooking juices and serve immediately.

VARIATION

You could also prepare young pheasant in the same way.

Red Mullet Fillets with Orecchiette, Amaretto & Orange Sauce

Serves 4

INGREDIENTS

90 g/3 oz/3³/₄ cup plain
   (all purpose) flour
8 red mullet fillets
25 g/1 oz/2 tbsp butter
150 ml/¹/₄ pint/⁵/₈ cup fish
   stock
1 tbsp crushed almonds
1 tsp pink peppercorns

1 orange, peeled and cut
   into segments
1 tbsp orange liqueur
grated rind of 1 orange
450 g/1 lb dried orecchiette
1 tbsp olive oil
150 ml/¹/₄ pint/⁵/₈ cup double
   (heavy) cream

4 tbsp amaretto
salt and pepper

TO GARNISH:
2 tbsp snipped fresh chives
1 tbsp toasted almonds

1 Season the flour and sprinkle into a shallow bowl. Press the fish fillets into the flour to coat. Melt the butter in a frying pan (skillet) and fry the fish over a low heat for 3 minutes, until browned.

2 Add the fish stock to the pan and cook for 4 minutes. Carefully remove the fish, cover with foil and keep warm.

3 Add the almonds, pink peppercorns, half the orange, the orange liqueur and orange rind to the pan. Simmer until the liquid has reduced by half.

4 Meanwhile, bring a large saucepan of lightly salted water to the boil. Add the orecchiette and olive oil and cook for 15 minutes, until tender but still firm to the bite.

5 Season the sauce and stir in the cream and amaretto. Cook for 2 minutes. Coat the fish with the sauce in the pan.

6 Drain the pasta and transfer to a serving dish. Top with the fish fillets and their sauce. Garnish with the remaining orange segments, the chives and toasted almonds. Serve.

Spaghetti al Tonno

Serves 4

INGREDIENTS

200 g/7 oz can tuna, drained
60 g/2 oz can anchovies,
    drained
250 ml/9 fl oz/1$^1/_8$ cups
    olive oil

60 g/2 oz/1 cup roughly
    chopped flat leaf parsley,
    plus extra to garnish
150 ml/$^1/_4$ pint/$^5/_8$ cup crème
    fraîche

450 g/1 lb dried spaghetti
25 g/1 oz/2 tbsp butter
salt and pepper
black olives, to garnish
crusty bread, to serve

1 Remove any bones from the tuna. Put the tuna into a food processor or blender, together with the anchovies, 225 ml/ 8 fl oz/1 cup of the olive oil and the flat leaf parsley. Process until smooth.

2 Spoon the crème fraîche into the food processor or blender and process again for a few seconds to blend thoroughly. Season to taste.

3 Bring a large pan of lightly salted water to the boil. Add the spaghetti

and the remaining olive oil and cook until tender, but still firm to the bite.

4 Drain the spaghetti, return to the pan and place over a medium heat. Add the butter and toss well to coat. Spoon in the sauce and quickly toss into the spaghetti, using 2 forks.

5 Remove the pan from the heat and divide the spaghetti between 4 warm individual serving plates. Garnish with olives and parsley and serve with warm, crusty bread.

VARIATION

If liked, you could add 1–2 garlic cloves to the sauce, substitute 25 g/ 1 oz/$^1/_2$ cup chopped fresh basil for half the parsley and garnish with capers instead of black olives.

Spaghetti with Smoked Salmon

Serves 4

INGREDIENTS

450 g/1 lb dried buckwheat
   spaghetti
2 tbsp olive oil
90 g/3 oz/$^1/_2$ cup crumbled
   feta cheese
salt

fresh coriander (cilantro) or
   parsley leaves, to garnish

SAUCE:
300 ml/$^1/_2$ pint/$1^1/_4$ cups
   double (heavy) cream
150 ml/$^1/_4$ pint/$^5/_8$ cup whisky
   or brandy

125 g/4$^1/_2$ oz smoked salmon
pinch of cayenne pepper
black pepper
2 tbsp chopped fresh coriander
   (cilantro) or parsley

1 Bring a large pan of lightly salted water to the boil. Add the spaghetti and 1 tbsp of the olive oil and cook until tender, but still firm to the bite. Drain and return to the pan with the remaining olive oil. Cover, set aside and keep warm.

2 Pour the cream into a small saucepan and bring to simmering point, but do not let it boil. Pour the whisky or brandy into another small saucepan and bring to simmering point, but do not allow it to boil. Remove both pans from the heat and mix together the cream and whisky or brandy.

3 Cut the smoked salmon into thin strips and add to the cream mixture. Season with cayenne and black pepper. Just before serving, stir in the fresh coriander (cilantro) or parsley.

4 Transfer the spaghetti to a warm serving dish, pour over the sauce and toss thoroughly with 2 large forks. Scatter over the crumbled feta cheese, garnish with the coriander (cilantro) or parsley leaves and serve immediately.

COOK'S TIP

Serve this rich and luxurious dish with a green salad tossed in a lemony dressing.